D1826268

ST. FRANCIS for TODAY

ST. FRANCIS
for TODAY

REV. FR. EDMUND O' GORMAN
OFM. Conv.

i

Copyright © 1987
REV. FR. EDMUND O'GORMAN
OFM. CONV.

ISBN/0 85342 836 0 – MERCIA PRESS LTD., CORK

ISBN/0 85244 130 4 – FOWLER WRIGHT BOOKS LTD., LEOMINSTER

This book is distributed in Ireland by:

Mercier Press Limited
Bridge Street, Cork.

Printed by
Davis Brothers, Leominster, Herefordshire.

CONTENTS

Pax et Bonum
Peace and Goodwill

FOREWORD

This short life of St. Francis is not meant to be a complete, critical or historical survey; rather particular steps in his life are brought before us, usually in historical sequence, but in some cases by bringing together events that fit together simply by topicality and proximity of thought.

It seems to me that the reading of the life of any saint ought not to be done in a spirit of criticism, but rather with a spirit of love and admiration, for our salvation is secured less by understanding and knowledge than by loving and doing.

Much that was done in the Middle Ages could hardly be done in the same way today. They make a grave mistake who transliterate St. Francis' life and ideals into the present century, and tend to look upon him as some sort of drop-out, a beatnik, a patron saint of tramps, a resister of authority. He was none of these things.

For this reason our story makes an application of a point in his life to your life today. A thought touching upon each chapter is suggested, an angle of personal betterment. A short examination of conscience would be a good follow-up, and this ought to lead to an increase of love and the commitment of some personal work of mercy or charity.

Each step of St. Francis' life would thus become part of yours.

SON OF BERNARDONE

In the twelth century people everywhere could be divided into certain well defined categories: priests, monks and nuns dedicated to the service of religion and humanity; nobles of greater or lesser degree, whose main occupation was the pursuit of military glory and the maintenance of family pride; and merchants, both those who operated only in the home markets and those, merchant venturers, who sought foreign fields of commerce. The remainder of the people were peasants, labourers and servants.

There was not a great deal of communication between one group and another. The nobles were exclusive by heredity; the merchants were self-contained by privilege; and only the Church was open to all classes and standards. The Gospel of Christ and the authority of the Church were the only principles common to all sections and in which all shared, and by which each was occasionally brought to heel.

This exclusiveness, however, was gradually being broken down. The princes, knights and military men, returning disappointed from the ill-fated Crusades, unwilling to forsake the only profession they knew, stirred up a spirit of political independence that led to strife between town and town, district and district. The merchant venturers, profiting from the opening up of the markets of the East, were travelling further afield in the promotion of their business. Among the upper class groups, the thinkers and the learned, under the light of new teachings and philosophies, were beginning to question many of the old truths, and were paving the way for the movement known as The Revival of Learning.

1

The world was, indeed, in a very unsettled state. Certainly, religious practices of centuries were still observed, but Christianity was not having the impact that it once had. Apart from the Cathedrals and the monastries, churches were derelict, and many of the people cared little for the love of Christ. Men's hearts had grown cold and a certain materialistic and indifferent attitude pervaded every section of society. There were, indeed, those in the Church who noted all this and tried their best to rectify it; and there were others, too, who in mis-guided zeal, plunged themselves into heresy because of it.

Towards the end of that century, in the year 1181, one of the merchant venturers of Assisi, a small hill town now a morning's journey north of Rome, was away in France on one of his business journeys. Pietro Bernardone must have said goodbye to his wife on that occasion with a certain apprehension, for he would have realized that the first child of the family would be born while he was away. He was a rather stern and dedicated business-man, who let nothing get in the way of his work. On the other hand, he always felt secure leaving his shop in the care of his wife, who was well able to look after it. So it would be now; she would manage no matter what happened.

As the sun set one evening in autumn Donna Pica left her friend's house, whom she had been visiting at the lower end of the town, and set out on her way home with a girl accompanying her. She was not well and leaned heavily on the girl as they trudged up through the flagged alleyways between the stone built houses. Now and again she stopped for a rest, but as they mounted near to the town square, she felt she could go no further and gently edged her companion into a nearby stable, saying that there they would rest for a while. It is said that in that place, on the straw,

2

a son was born to Pietro Bernardone's wife. Born, like Christ, in a stable!

In due course the baby was taken by a nurse and the god-parents to be baptized at the Cathedral of San Rufino. There he received his name John, almost a prophetic name for this child, who, like his patron, was to smooth the way for the Gospel of Christ.

About the same time that the son of the merchant was baptized, the son of a very illustrious prince was brought to the same font. Frederick, the son of Henry, the German prince who resided at the Castle of Assisi, arrived to the blare of trumpets and the panopy of minor royalty. But what a divergence as the two children grew to manhood! The one became a humble preacher and a saint; the other a proud, irreligious man and a renegade.

On the way back from the baptism the Bernardone party met an old and enquiring pilgrim. He seemed to come from nowhere, but he wanted to hold the baby - at least for a second or two. The nurse was very reluctant, but at his gentle insistence and his kindly attitude, she placed the little bundle in his arms. As he hugged the little one close his old face lit up with great joy. He blessed him and said to those who stood by: "I say to you that this little child will live to do great things for God, honour and reverence will follow his name wherever it is mentioned". He handed little John back to the nurse and vanished in the side streets.

By a peculiar quirk of circumstances, however, the child was never to be known as John. When Pietro returned, overjoyed at a very successful business venture in France, he sought to perpetuate this wordly success by dubbing the baby France, or Francis - an uncommon, but not unknown name at the time. And so the child of Pietro Bernardone and Donna Pica has always been known as Francis of Assisi.

ALL MEN EQUAL?

Born in a stable or in palace, in a slum or in a villa, in a country cottage or in a city dwelling; is there any difference? There is indeed, and in some cases insurmountable differences. One of the greatest fallacies ever broached is the assertion that all men are born equal. The opposite is the truth.

We are all born equal in only one way, and that is by the second birth, the birth into divine love and grace by baptism. Prince or peasant, rich or poor, learned or unlearned, healthy or deformed, all start with the same opportunity for salvation. Christ loves each individually with an equally intense love and all are equally destined for eternal happiness. The words of Pope Pius X, a member of the Secular Franciscan Order, are to the point: "The equality existing among the various social members consists only in this: that all men have their origin in God, their Creator, have been redeemed by Jesus Christ, and are to be judged and rewarded or punished by God exactly according to their merits or demerits." (Letters, 1903).

What do you think about all this? Are you envious of others? Do you sometimes regret that your parents were not resident in some baronial mansion; that they were perhaps not upper middle class, that they were not as intelligent or learned as some others? These are envious and futile thoughts; each of us has his own particular advantages, and the great

4

truth is that only at the baptismal font is everyone equal. Happiness in life will be the surer if from the start we can instil such divine content into the soul, instead of growing through life in a spirit of contention, trying to beat the other person to a noble prestige, a business advantage, or a higher position of some kind or another. There is no room in Christianity for resentment at class or other distinctions.

**Most High, Most Gracious
Good Lord**

**To Thee Belong Praise, Honour, Glory
And Every Blessing**

THE BOY AND THE HOME

The Bernardone household was very much a maternal domain. Pietro, the merchant, was frequently away travelling in the course of his business, and consequently Francis grew up more under the influence of a good and pious mother, and less under that of his equally good but nevertheless worldy-minded father. Donna Pica was one of those great ladies, ladies in the finest sense of the term, who trained their offspring to love God above all things and human beings for His sake.

Thus Francis grew up at his mother's knee, learning his own language and at the same time grasping onto her native French as well; delighting in the stories she told him of romance, chivalry and troubadours, so much so, indeed, that the knightly ideals of honour, courtesy and religious dedication from the stories of Roland, Arthur of the Round Table and others, characterized him all his life. The small school by the church of St. George is where he received his first formal education and learned Latin.

The periods when his father was at home were times of stark reality to Francis. From him he learned, and he was an apt pupil in this, the facts of the business world, how to buy and sell and barter. As he grew into his teens he readily took his place in the family business and no doubt travelled to nearby towns selling the cloth and tapestries. Perhaps on occasion he even travelled to France with his father. Pietro was delighted and proud to see his son assuming a position in the business and a place of notability in the life of the town, and so he left much responsibility to him.

But if Francis was growing to be a good market man, he was also a bit of a spendthrift. He could drive a good bargain, but he had a soft heart. We can imagine his mother reproving him for this defect. She prayed and gently guided him, and when someone complained to her of Francis' spendthrift behaviour, she contented herself by observing: "All the same, I always hope that he will turn out a real child of God after all."

During his years at the shop an incident occurred that made a deep impression on him. Francis was naturally kind and courteous, but one day a beggar came in and interrupted some important work, asking for alms for the love of God. No doubt unthinkingly he repulsed him and told him to be off. As the poor man turned the corner of the street, a great remorse fell upon Francis; held back by the cares of business and a certain greed for profit, he had refused alms to a beggar. He accused himself of great churlishness, saying; "If that poor man had asked something for the sake of a great count or baron, you would surely have given him what he asked for. How much more, therefore, should you have done this for the name of the King of Kings and the Lord of All!" He determined never to refuse anything in the name of so great a Lord.

From that time on, when there was only himself and his mother at home, Francis took to laying the table in grand style as if for many people. His mother wondered why he was always putting out so many loaves on the table, and he told her that it was in case any of the poor should knock at the door and ask help in the name of God. She thought much about these peculiarities of his, but she did not interfere with him.

In those days there was a certain simpleton around the streets of Assisi, who, whenever he met Francis, would take off his cloak and put it down in the road before him, saying that thus he wished to salute and acknowledge a man who was destined to do great things and be praised and honoured by all Christians. Certainly Francis Bernardone was flattered; he was rich, a society man well known about town and in business - of course he would do great things!

PARENTAL INFLUENCE

Parents sometimes make either of two mistakes in bringing up their children. They love them too much, or they love them too little. They over-protect and cocoon them, or they show little concern and leave them to their own devices. Both are decidedly wrong. A growing child must develop under a restraint, guided but not repressive; under a solicitude but not cotton-wooling.

Traditionally one sympathises with a child tied to its mother's apron strings, or continually under its father's shadow. Such children are never permitted to go out and about on their own, to join other children in clubs, societies or organizations; even going to church must necessarily be a family affair keeping apart from others. It seems they must never think for themselves, but meekly follow every parental whim and fancy. Over protectionism is the key-note. No wonder when they get into their teens they round on their protectors, kick over the traces, and are off.

On the other hand there are those parents, affectionate enough, but who treat their children as some sort of excess baggage - "latch-key children". Home to them is simply somewhere to sleep, to have a meal - though that can be done equally as well elsewhere.

They are not, as might be at first thought, children of poorer families. This afflicts all classes of society. In many cases the father works far more hours than he needs to, and so to his children he is a passing figure. Mother, too, under a mistaken idea of self fulfilment, or perhaps to keep the car on the road or secure holidays abroad, is likewise out of the house most of the day, while the children are left in a nursery or simply to their own devices. In some few cases both parents may be impelled to this sort of living by necessity, but in most cases it is not so. It is the child who has to be considered, and parents' first duty is to provide companionship and look after their children; other things are quite secondary. Leaving children to their own devices or in the care of others, lack of parental proximity, care and supervision in the early formative years are surely the cause of a lot of our vandalism.

Donna Pica fell into neither of these traps. We can sense in the little we know about her, that she exerted a firm but gentle guidance. While she impressed on Francis the necessity of right living, honouring God and loving one's neighbour, he was yet left free, coming and going among his equals in Assisi, and thus learning slowly from experience what his mother inculcated by percept. It is the only way. A steady guidance by example and without repression.

The Second Vatican Council reminds us: "For it is the parents' task to create the kind of family atmosphere, inspired by love and by piety towards God and men, that is favourable to the complete personal and social education of their children. The family, then, is the first school of those social virtues that every society needs. But it is most important in the

Christian family, enriched by grace and the obligations of the Sacrament of Matrimony, that children must be taught right from infancy to know and worship God according to the faith they received in Baptism, and to love their neighbour. There, too, they meet with their first experience of sound, human society and of the Church." (Christian Education).

Praise Ye, Bless Ye, My Lord

**Give Him Thanks And Serve Him
With Great Humility**

SOLDIERING AND SICKNESS

The days of Francis' youth were days of intermittent war, or rather, local skirmishes. All this hardly concerns us, but there is no doubt that Francis Bernardone took his expected place in these forays.

In 1202 a sharp engagement took place between the Assisians and the Perugians. The great bell at the town square boomed out over the countryside calling all the young gallants and nobles. Francis, who was accepted among them as a successful merchant and a good leader, also sallied forth on a charger fittingly caparisoned. The battle took place at Ponte San Giovanni. We do not know very much about it, but the men of Assisi lost, and their leaders, including Francis, found themselves in a dungeon in Perugia.

The idleness and restrictions of prison life grated on the men's nerves, and living became a sort of cat-and-dog life. One man in particular made himself obnoxious to the rest; all avoided him, except Francis who slowly gained his confidence, sweetened his temper and reconciled him to his fellows. Francis himself had also come in for a great deal of criticism because he appeared to take the whole affair very lightly. The fact is that he naturally had a bright outlook on life and this stood him in good stead. After all, was he not the acknowledged leader of the revels and the young social life in his home town? Obviously he felt it his duty to try to cheer them up with his snatches of songs and ballads.

"You are acting like a mad man," said one of them, "to be happy even in prison."

"It doesn't really matter what you think of me," answered Francis, "I shall become famous all over the world."

After about a year they were all back in Assisi, everything forgotten, and taking part again in the nightly revels. The leader, however, seemed to be no longer as whole heartedly involved as he once had been. He kept becoming reflective and dropping behind. They shouted to him: "What's the matter? What are you dreaming about that you keep dropping behind?" Then another taunted: "Thinking of taking a wife?" To which Francis called back: "That's it; that's the truth. But I have in mind a bride richer and nobler than you ever saw!"

Later Francis fell gravely ill with fever and had to spend many months in bed. He only recovered slowly, and then found his way about with a stick. Much time was spent meditatively looking out over the Umbrian plain, a view that had once given him much joy, but now seemed to be barren and gave him no inspiration. His pattern of life somehow seemed to be wrong and he was passing through a worried period of self examination.

In 1205 once again the bugles blew and the drums beat and all the valiants and nobles turned out to enrol under the banner of a famous general, Walter of Brienne, who was fighting the battles of the Pope against the Emperor. Francis was strong now and he took this as his opportunity. This was, indeed, a noble action against foreigners and usurpers, not against one's own kith and kin like the Perugia affray; this it was that was to bring him a great name and make him famous. Pietro Bernardone was overjoyed at his son's readiness for military prowess, and fitted him out in grand style as became a merchant's son who was now to ride out with the finest flower of knighthood.

In the course of these preparations Francis experienced a very vivid dream or vision. It seemed that he rode up to a grand castle and entered the large baronial hall. There appeared to be no one around, but the walls of the hall were covered with weapons, suits of armour, plumed helmets and all the accoutrements of war. It was all very splendid and obviously prepared for a legion of knights. Almost involuntarily he exclaimed aloud in admiration: "For whom are all these thing prepared?" And a quiet, firm voice seemed to answer: "All this that you see is yours; all belongs to you and your knights!" Indeed, it all fitted in very well with his plans: a period of service in the field, then a knighthood, eventually a position as general or leader of men.

He was at the very peak of enthusiasm when he rode out from Assisi in grand style with Walter of Brienne amid the cheers of the citizens, the blare of trumpets and the fluttering of flags and pennants. But the excitement was too great and Francis under-estimated his health. As the army drew near to Spoleto he fell ill with a touch of fever and had to be left behind. As he lay ill he could see the ideal of military glory being filched away from him; he was in a state of perplexity.

While in this state it seemed to him that he heard a voice posing the question: "Who is it better to serve, the master or the servant?"

When the question was repeated, Francis answered unhesitatingly: "Certainly the Master!"

"Then," continued the voice, "Why do you leave God who is the Master to serve man who is the servant?"

"O Lord," he answered, "what must I do?"

Return to your own place, and there it will be shown you what you are to do."

THE WORLD OF IDEALS

St. Francis was from the start a person of great ideals; his sights were aimed high no matter on what course he set himself. He rose to be the leader of the youth at Assisi, he led the way among the town merchants, and he set himself to become a leader in military prowess. He reached out always for the highest and the best.

We must all be people of ideals and we must all aim high. In fact there is little trouble about this, because most of us, especially when young, do have high ideals. If there is trouble, it starts from the fact that we imagine we are the only people engaged in this particular quest. As the years go by there are many others who come into the picture for better or for worse; and, above all, there is always Almighty God Himself.

Whilst we must be firm in our resolve and movement towards an ideal, yet we must understand that the ideal itself, since it is in the future, must remain flexible. It is a very foolish thing to meet a grave obstacle and to go on bashing one's head against a stone wall. After due perseverance we should be ready to recognize that perhaps the finger of God is pointing in another direction; that we should quieten down and examine our motives. The prudent realization of the will of God giving direction through the ordinary events of life is essential. In the battle of life God is the Supreme Commander, as Francis came to understand. His directions are surely to be unquestionably obeyed.

The Abbe de Tourville says: "This great and glorious condition of life which makes us liken it, not perhaps to a battle, but to a battle field on which we do not know who will be struck down or how: this should determine us to show the simple courage of the true soldier, resigned, yet never downcast or gloomy. In this respect you are trained for war, since you have seen so many of those whom you have loved struck down. Of those who have left you such happy memories, say, as they say in the army, 'They died on the field of honour'. We are sent to it by God, and we are not recalled from it except by Him. On it we experience all the hardships, all the loneliness, all the difficulties, and also all the unnoticed and trivial heroisms which are met with so often on military expeditions and which go to make up the qualities of the soldier. Let us then go forward and accept this hard but glorious condition of our life." (Letters)

You are a member of the Church Militant - or, as they like to say now - the Church Pilgrimaging. Are you under willing obedience to your Divine Commander, or do you resent His orders? Is obedience only given when it corresponds with your own will and ideals? Do you bash ahead with your own self-opinionated ideas without recognizing His hand in your affairs? If so, then you are slowly heading for a state of frustration and nervous upset. Better to stop and consider the will of God unravelling itself in ordinary, everyday events and act accordingly.

THE TRIPLE RENUNCIATION

How was he to settle himself in life? This was Francis' big question. He had felt drawn towards the glamour and renown of soldiering, but seemingly this was not meant for him; the ideal of a merchant, for a nature so expansive, became increasingly repellent because of its grasping and money-consciousness. The voice of God calling to nobler things was speaking quietly within him and his better nature was slowly following. But it was all so very indecisive for a lively young man who wanted action. Then the solution came to him: a pilgrimage to Rome for guidance.

It was June 1205 that Francis first arrrived in the Eternal City. To the young merchant from the hill town it was all very inspiring and grand. The multiplicity of churches, the solemn ceremonies, the sound of various languages spoken by pilgrims from all the known world, the grandeur of St. Peter's itself, and all the external trappings of the Church that transcended the frontiers of time and space, the one sure guide in the pilgrimage of life.

Francis prayed at the tomb of the Apostle, attended Mass, took advices from spiritual men, and stood and watched as successions of pilgrims threw their offerings into the enclosure reserved for that purpose. He contrasted the wealth and pomp of some of them with the pittance they gave; it pained and shocked him to see so many well dressed and obviously affluent persons acting so niggardly. He stepped forward, and putting his hand into his satchel a few times, he flung his whole supply of money with a resounding clash into the offertory area. Everyone was startled and looked round, but Francis walked off unperturbed. He possessed nothing now, except his grand clothing; he was a practical pauper and would have to beg like the rest of them. It was his first great renunciation.

Going out from the great basilica, he passed through the ranks of beggars of all descriptions who lined the way with appealing cries and outstretched palms. He had made one great renunciation - he had broken with money; another now faced him - renunciation of a comfortably established way of life. Francis respectfully approached one of the beggar men, took his hand and astonished him by suggesting that they should change clothes. The startled man had never heard of such an offer and immediately agreed. He skipped away, delighted in Francis's fine clothes, whilst the young society man, clad in the old flea-ridden rags, took his place amongst the crowd of motley merchants. How many days he stayed among them, begging his crusts we don't know, but he had now became a really poor man and as such he returned home begging his bread on the way. He realized at last what it meant to be "a poor man of God." He had released himself from the tyranny of money and status. One other triumph had yet to come.

Back in Assisi his father saw to it that he was once again well and finely clothed, and he no doubt received some harsh words about his new way of life and about family standards. Like the rich he also had a horse to ride and he spent a lot of time riding alone around the countryside. During one of these meditative trips an incident occurred which was his third renunciation - the third purification of character.

Francis met a leper. He was, indeed, always sympathetic and kind to the sick and the poor, but he had an ingrained fear and aversion to lepers. Even the district of the leper hospital about a mile from Assisi was pestilential to him and he never went near it. So he stopped his horse at some distance. Ordinarily he would have flung a few coins at the man and made off, but this time his frame of mind was quite changed. He dismounted, approached the timid leper and greeted him as a brother. He kissed the diseased hand and gave the expected money, and then - what was unheard of - he embraced him and they exchanged the kiss of peace. He then watched as the suffering man returned to the lazaretto. He gazed after him, then he summed up his courage and he followed and committed himself to looking after these poor and repulsive outcasts. It was a great psychological triumph over his own nature.

"When I lived in sin, it was very painful to me to see lepers," wrote St. Francis later, "but God led me into their midst and I remained there for a little while. When I left them, that which had seemed to me bitter had become sweet and easy."

"LET HIM RENOUNCE HIMSELF"

Renunciation is not a word we like. It implies self-denial and that likewise is not particularly welcome. But there comes a time in everyone's life when we must renounce something. It may happen because of trouble of some kind, business reverses. Something has to be given up in order to meet creditors or to keep ourselves solvent. It may be annual holidays abroad, perhaps dining out and theatre going, perhaps some cherished valuable object has to be got rid of. All this is unavoidable renunciation, which can be faced in bad grace or good grace, and might just as well, for peace of soul, be faced with the latter disposition. We all admire a person who meets misfortune with resignation, settles his affairs, picks up the traces and ploughs on again.

18

But there is a far nobler "giving up", or change of habits that can characterize us. This comes quite voluntarily. Like St. Francis we all become set in certain patterns of life, certain activity, not bad in itself but inconsequential. If we thought things over we might find that we could do far better with our lives and property and the time left to us; we could "renounce" for the sake of Christ and the Gospel.

The Church in her parishes needs ready and willing workers who might deny themselves an evening or two a week in order to engage in charitable work. There is also ecumenical activity, which may not be particularly pleasurable to some but which gives pleasure to others and increases their knowledge and appreciation of the Church. Essentially it is a giving of oneself, time and attention to others. Francis gave himself to the beggars and the lepers.

St. Jerome, writing to certain Christian ladies in Rome, tells them: "I know well that many of the rich show mercy to the poor, but they do so by the hands of others. They give their gold, but not their personal services, because the sight of misery inspires disgust and makes them ill. I will not find fault with this weakness, nor will I call it unmerciful. But I must be allowed to say that true love and perfect faith raise the mind above such infirmities and make it strong for holy services of love."

**When Will Men Understand That
Without His Spirit of Brotherliness
And Love, It Is Quite
Impossible To Have Peace?**

REPAIR MY CHURCH

The old man in Francis was dead. The spiritual hero in him was pressing forward. He was waiting for some sort of decisive call from God. This came in a way he least expected, and in the first instance it was not recognized in its true importance.

In travelling around the countryside Francis had developed a habit of praying and meditating in the often uncared for small churches. He himself tells us: "Our Lord gave me such a lively faith and love for churches that I used to adore Him in these words, 'We adore Thee, O Lord Jesus Christ, here and in all thy churches throughout the world, and we bless Thee, because by thy holy Cross Thou hast redeemed the world.'"

One Autumn afternoon in 1206 Francis was praying ardently in the small, almost derelict church of St. Damian in the valley below Assisi. He was kneeling at a small alter before an ancient Byzantine Crucifix. Uppermost in his mind was the great love of the Saviour who died that supreme happiness might be ours. Suddenly as he raised his head, it seemed that the figure of Our Lord spoke to him: "Francis, go and repair my church, which, as you see, is falling into ruins." He was startled and a bit frightened, but when the voice was heard a second and a third time, the command was clear. It was to be accepted as given.

He looked around the little church. It was, indeed, in a very dilapidated state. It was up to him to do something about it. Stones would be necessary, and besides what could be found round about, others would be necessary. They would have to be bought and that meant money, and for some time now he had little regard for that commodity. Outside he met the

21

priest who said Mass there occasionally. He emptied his pockets to him, telling him to buy oil and keep a lamp burning before the Crucifix.

Francis still had his horse, and he mounted it and rode to Assisi, straight to his father's shop. Taking down various rolls of cloth from the shelves, he bundled them together, strapped them to the horse, and quickly made off for the town of Foligno. The merchant's son from Assisi was well known in the market place, and there he secured a good price for the merchandize. That, however, was not all. The horse, too, was worth money, so that was sold as well. As on a former occasion the young Assisian had walked back from Rome, so now he walked back from Foligno, a beggar once again.

At the ruined church of St. Damian he found the priest-in-charge and gave him the money, requesting that it be used to repair the building for the poor. The priest looked askance at it; he was very suspicious and refused to have anything to do with it. Francis thereupon threw it onto the window-sill and left it there.

He had by now almost severed his ties with home. His father's house and business was not the place where he wished to spend his life. He was poor now and he wished to remain so. The little church was to be the centre of his immediate work - "repair my church" - and he persuaded the old priest that he could help him greatly to put the church in good order, and for this reason to let him live there.

Meanwhile he was not unknown in the town, for he went round collecting stones from the citizens and wheeling them away in a barrow. His former friends were astonished and some were quite rude to him; others simply looked on it all as a young man's passing peculiarity and laughed it off. He weathered them all,

22

going from street to street begging: "He who gives me one stone," he said "shall have one reward; he who gives me three shall have that number of rewards." It was very simple language, and purposely so, for he had set himself against the complexities and superfluities of life about him.

On one of these trips he came to a house he knew well where they spoke French. They were engaged in a game, so they did not see him approach. As he got near the door, he suddenly felt ashamed and turned away. Then he stopped. That was a grave fault, thought he, and immediately went back, walked into the group and asked for alms to keep the lamps burning at St. Damian's.

The young quasi-hermit was fond of French, which was the language of his mother, and he used to use this language in shouting to passers-by: "Come and help me in the work at St. Damian's."

One such person asked him: "Come and help - why?"

"Because this shall become the monastery of Ladies whose fame and life shall glorify our Heavenly Father in the universal Church."

CARING LAITY AND CARE OF THE CHURCH

The Catholic church is the house of God. It is the house of God in a very special way, and in this it differs from other churches that are not Catholic. God Himself lives in our churches under the form of bread, the Second Person of the Blessed Trinity. In the tabernacle He is as actually present with us as He was at Nazareth and Bethany. How well kept then ought to be the home of the Saviour! "I have loved, O Lord, the glory of thy house."

St. Francis deemed it a great honour and privilege to repair and keep clean the houses of God. Generations of Catholics in all countries have thought with the mind of St. Francis; men and women have contributed their talents and labour to continually beautifying and cleaning the church.

Alas, that this fine spirit should appear to be dying out! Many older people can surely remember the times when painters, carpenters, joiners, gardeners and others were always ready to give of their talents and free time to church work; teams of dedicated ladies worked week about to scrub (in those days), dust, tidy and polish in church and sacristy. Alas indeed, that this spirit of love and dedication appears to be passing! While there are still a few churches where the old spirit prevails, the most of them are now treated as any common factory or office block, where paid workers do their stint. If you pay, the work will be done; otherwise not. Suggest a practical job to the average lay person and the first reaction is that there is no time. A remoter, unexpressed consideration is how much is the job worth. People seem to have plenty of time to sit on councils, go conferencing, natter interminably on committees, but little time to dedicate to any active, down-to-earth work around the church or its grounds. It's all a great shame.

What about your own parish church, or some poorer church not too far distant? are we ready to sit back in our modernly equipped, fully carpeted and highly decorated homes and watch the house of God go dirty and shabby? Are the men in the parish so frightfully busy every hour of the week, that they stand by and watch lawns go wild, hedges go untrimmed and weeds flourish around God's house? All perhaps because the priest has not the money to dispose for hired help. Look around your parish church and grounds and see if it is a credit to the parishioners or a living accusation of parochial disinterest.

Even if the priest had all the money in the world, what about the honour and the privilege of acting in the manner of St. Francis? "Go and repair my church." Examine your conscience and commit yourself to some active work around your church or church grounds. If you have the health, you know quite well that you can find the time, if you want to give God a share.

Blesssed Be Thou, My Lord

For Our Sisters, Moon And Stars:
Formed In The Heavens
Fair And Clear

BREAK WITH FAMILY TIES

Pietro Bernardone arrived back from his travels to find Francis no longer at home. He was living a very simple life at St. Damian's and shunning society. The father was furious and went in high dudgeon to the town authorities. Forgetful that his son was now a young man of twenty-five, he demanded that he be brought back under the parental roof. The town councillors might have tried to disuade an ordinary citizen, but this rich merchant, Bernardone, was someone to reckon with, so they were prepared to do what they could to please him. A group of vigilants were dispatched to St. Damian's to bring Francis home.

They surely must have expected the obvious response: "The authorities at Assisi know that I am now a committed servant of God and I am no longer under their jurisdiction. This little church of St. Damian, the church of the miraculous Crucifix, belongs to the Bishop of Assisi; it is a holy place and here I take asylum and my person is inviolable."

Very well, then, if that was the way Francis wanted it, he would be cited before the Church authorities. Bishop Guido the Second of Assisi therefore set a date and time and ordered the father and son and counsellors to come before him. One cold December afternoon in 1206 the father faced his son across the court assembled at the episcopal palace. Many merchants, knights and common people were also there to witness this extraordinary affair.

Pietro Bernardone started in a sentimental way, remarking that this was his son who had run away. He was older than his brother and so would succeed to the business, and would be his support in his old age. There were nods of assent and agreement, but nothing decisive came from the Bishop. As the father rambled on he became more heated and bitter, and accused Francis of throwing his money away on ruined churches, stealing a bolt of cloth from his warehouse, selling his expensive horse, and generally being a thorough going disgrace to his family and to the town - in other words, he was convinced that he was not in his right mind and needed care.

Eventually the Bishop rose from his chair: "Francis," he said, "you have heard what you father has said; he is certainly very angry with you. I suggest that you give him back any money that you still have, and then place yourself onto the inexhaustible riches of God."

"My Lord and father of us all," answered Francis, "I readily restore what money I have," and he handed over his wallet, "but more than this, he can have also the very clothes on my back - they are his." At this he began to divest himself, and somebody ran out and came back with a sack and a rope. This was hastily placed over him and tied in with the rope - the first Franciscan habit! Gathering up his clothes, he then proffered them to his father, and turning to the assembled people, said: "Listen to me and pay attention: up to this moment I have called Pietro Bernardone my father; from now on, despoiled of everything, I can say with greater conviction "Our Father, who art in heaven." The father grabbed the bundle of clothes, disinherited his son, and strode out in great anger. It was probably the last Francis saw of him.

HINDRANCE OR HELP?

It used to be the case in very many families that the sons followed their fathers in business or profession, or at least they had their life mapped out for them by their parents, who understood that this guidance was necessary. Nowadays, however it is pretty much the case that young people map their own and form their own life. Parents maintain a low profile and a discreet guidance. Strangely there is one choice that modern parents are reluctant to allow their children to make. It is the spirit of Pietro Bernardone in a modern concept. Let a boy or a girl mention that they wish to dedicate their lives to the Church and immediately there are insinuated objections. Seldom is there much encouragement. At its most selfish the question is what about the family name? At its most objective the principle is - think again. Why segregate oneself from others? Move about in the world a bit and then make a decision, in any case, one can do a great deal of good in the world as a Catholic lay person. The idea with many people seems to be that the good Lord must not have the first choice or claim on one's talents and life, but He can come along as a secondary consideration!

The Church is short of priests, Brothers, Sisters and Nuns. How much of this is due to the selfishness of parents, who are not ready to allow a child to make its own choice and follow God's call? They detrimentally interfere when they ought to constructively encourage. The seeds of a vocation are set in the hearts of many children and young people, but through lack of encouragement are then stiffled as the child grows. Delay in acceptance often means that the spirit of the world creeps in and another vocation is lost. Let no parent act like Pietro Bernardone; but when the grace is given, foster and develop it and there may be another St. Francis.

Blessed Be Thou, My Lord

**For Our Sister Water, Very useful,
Humble, Chaste And Precious**

THE FIRST FRIARS

The affair at the Bishop's palace became the talk of the town. The like had never been heard of before. Opinion among the citizens was divided, some thought Francis was suffering from an illness, others agreed that he was truly a man of God. Almong these latter there was a certain good-living knight, Bernard of Quintavalle, probably one of Francis' former companions, a rich and influential man who admired his compatriot for his courage and action. He was not given to jumping to conclusions or being unduly swayed, and so in order to test Francis' change of life at first hand, he invited him to come and stay with him. During the night he watched his visitor and only pretended to sleep. Francis, not knowing that he was being observed, spent the night kneeling on the floor in intense prayer. By the time morning dawned Bernard had definitely made up his mind, and he said: "Brother Francis, I am wholly purposed in my heart to leave the world and to follow you in whatever way you may bid me." Together they then attended Mass at the Bishop's chapel and so sealed the contract.

On the way back they were overtaken by a canon of the Cathedral, Peter Cattani, who expressed a wish to join them. All canons in those days were not necessarily priests, and Peter was a layman or, perhaps, a minor cleric. He was not a rich man, but he was very clever and was a Doctor of Laws. He accepted the first condition, which was told him by St. Francis: "Give all you have to the poor, and come, follow Our Lord Jesus Christ."

It was Bernard, of course, who had most to dispose of, and for this purpose he engaged people to help him. One of these, a man recently returned to Assisi, Giles, was so moved at the sight of these wealthy and honoured men giving away their goods to the poor, that, as soon as the work was finished, he hastened to the church of St. George, and there before the Blessed Sacrament he spent some hours in prayer. He rose from his knees with the firm conviction that he, too, must join the Franciscan Brethren. Giles came to be renowned for obedience, humility and spiritual advices. He said: "The fear of God is holy and constrains men to submit themselves in true humility to the yoke of obedience and to bow their heads to the very earth. Humility is the daughter of the fear of God."

While Bernard was disposing of his property, a certain priest named Sylvester, who had sold stones to St. Francis when he was repairing churches, came up and complained: "Francis, you did not pay me well for the stones you had from me."

Without any comment Francis put his hand into Bernard's cloak and drew out a handful of money, which he gave to the priest. He did this a second time and then asked: "Are you paid in full, Sir Priest?"

"I am paid now in full, Brother," said he as he went happily away. In the course of the next few days, however, he began to consider remorsefully on his meanness. "Am I not a wretch, seeing that I am an old man and covet temporal things, while this young man despises and abhors them for the love of God?" Full of penitence with himself and admiration for the Brethren, he came to them and asked to be admitted to their company. He was the first priest in the Order.

And so they came - the followers of the little poor man. Concerning them, and to encourage them, Francis one day told them of a vision he had: "Comfort, my dear sons, and by joyful in the Lord; and distress not yourselves because to your eyes we appear to be but a few in number," and then he told them

31

how he had seen the future and great crowds flocking to the Franciscan way of life: "The French came, the Spaniards hurried, the Germans and the English ran, while others of diverse and unknown tongues pressed hard upon these, truly a multitude innumerable. Let us therefore return thanks to the almighty God."

THE POWER OF EXAMPLE

It would hardly be correct to say that the Franciscan Order was 'founded': it just grew. Neither did St. Francis ever ask anyone to join him: they just came. What was it, then, that made so many follow his way of life? Quite simply it was good example. Bernard came because he admired both; Giles was edified by Bernard's generosity, and the priest, Sylvester, was shamed by the Gospel witness given by the little group.

There is no doubt that much is done for good or evil by example; much more than by word. People are great imitators. The silent, continued reptition of a good or charitable act makes observers think, and from this thinking comes action. One hears of non-Catholics who became interested in the Church because of the Sunday morning regularity of their Catholic neighbours. Many children remain good and loyal because of the example of good parents; how many there are who slip away from the Faith because of the bad example of those who ought to edify them? And so it goes on through all aspects of life.

One thing we may take to mind is that we may never know the good we do by our example. Only very seldom does anyone mention the influence of example. As the ancient poet, Homer, said so long ago: "Let noble acts more noble acts inspire," and as St. Francis himself said, "Let us not fail in doing good, and in due course we shall reap life everlasting."

Blessed Be Thou My Lord

With All Thy Creatures

THE GOSPEL INJUNCTION

St. Francis was not exactly an organizer. He was not even yet quite clear as to his own future life and work; and now others were coming to him and expecting spiritual direction. The sources of all Catholic life and movement are Holy Scripture, tradition and the teaching authority of the Church, and this Francis well understood. Particularly was he a reverent lover of the Word of God. He naturally, therefore went to the Bible for his inspiration. This first came to him at St. Damian's, when he heard a particular piece of the Gospel read during Mass: "Take nothing with you to use on your journey, staff or wallet, or bread or money; you are not to have more than one coat apiece . . . So they set out and passed through the villages, preaching the Gospel and healing the sick wherever they went." (Luke 9, 3-7).

Obviously some minimum form of regulations had to be found for his little company, so on April 16th, 1208 he took Bernard of Quintavalle and Peter Cattani and went to the little church of St. Nicholas. Here they stayed for a long time in prayer, invoking the Holy Spirit, and then Francis approached the altar and, in the name of the Holy Trinity, opened the missal three times. At the first instance he read to them: "If thou hast a mind to be perfect, go home and sell all that belongs to thee; give it to the poor, and so the treasure that thou hast shall be in heaven; then come back and follow me." (Matt. 19.21). He closed the book, then slowly opened it again at another place, and from the line where his finger rested, he read out: "Take nothing with you to use on your journey, etc.," the same words he had heard previously at St. Damian's. A third time he opened the missal, and

the text under his finger was: "If any man has a mind
to come to my way, let him renounce self and take up
his cross and follow Me." (Matt. 16.24). "Brothers,"
said Francis, "this Christ commands of us. This must
be our life, based on the Gospel, and the life of all
those who might wish to join us. Go now, and put into
practice what you have heard!"

The three companions found a ruined and dis-
used hut in the plain below St. Damian's, by a twisty
little brook from which it was called Rivo-torto. This
they repaired and made into their home- the first
Franciscan Friary.

Later in life, when he was very ill and in great
pain, one of the brethren, seeking to console him,
advised him to have recourse to the Holy Scripture. "I
pray thee, now, also to have something read to thee
from the Prophets, and perhaps thy spirit will rejoice
in the Lord." He answered: "It is good to read the tes-
timonies of Scripture; it is good to seek out our Lord
God in them; but for myself I have already mastered
so much of the Scriptures that I have an ample store
for meditation and reflection. I need no more, my
son; I know Christ, poor and crucified."

STUDY OF THE BIBLE

One of the happy signs in this twentieth century
is a distinct turning of people to Holy Scripture. In
itself this is an excellent thing, but it is apt to get out
of proportion. The Catholic Church has always encouraged us to read the Bible, and she presents three
readings to us, as well as psalms, in every Sunday
Mass, which might well form our meditation for the
week. The priest is admonished to preach on these
readings - the homily. It is under obedience to the
holy Church that Catholics read and study Scripture.
Without this obedience we will find that "many men

have many minds" and so confusion and conflict is generated. Every one of the non-Catholic forms of Christianity will claim the Bible as its rule of faith! The Bible only was the great cry against the Church at the Reformation.

Therefore it would be a good thing to seek out a Catholic Bible study group and join it, and we can be sure of correct interpretation and right doctrine. On the other hand we must also be ecumenical in this, especially since our brethren in Christ are very strong on this point and almost every church group will have a bible class. We must be discreet in making our choice, and we cannot go far wrong if we stand by the recognized forms of Christianity - The Anglicans, Methodists, Baptists, Congregationalists, etc., remembering, of course, that in certain few things their teaching is not correct from the Catholic perspective - we can think of the words of Christ at the Last Supper, of his words of founding the Church upon St. Peter. To join in with them adds encouragement to good people and also develops our knowledge of the Bible, and adds to our Christian fellowship. On the other hand, we must be careful to avoid the bible fanatics - the "Armageddon round the corner," and the "I'm saved, the rest are damned," types. Arrogant Bible punching helps nobody. Truth must march at the side of spirituality.

St. Francis himself told us that when some brethren asked him about Bible study: "It pleases me well, provided however, that according to Christ's example, of whom it is written that he prayed more than he read, they omit not the study of prayer. Nor let them study merely in order to know how they ought to speak, but in order that they may do the things they have heard, and when they have done them set them before others to do. I wish my brethren to be disciples of the Gospel, and so to profit in knowledge of the truth that they may grow in the purity of simplicity, and not divide the simplicity of the dove from the wisdom of the serpent, which our most excellent Master has by his blessed mouth joined together." (Bonaventure x1.1).

Blessed Be Thou My Lord

**For My Brother The Wind, The Air,
For Cloud And Calm,
For Every Kind of Weather**

THE RULE OF LIFE

It was in that cramped wattle hut at Rivo-torto that the first germ of a Rule showed itself. In that place others came to join the original three companions, and it wasn't long before they intimated to Francis that it would be a good thing if they had some regulations regarding their form of life, amplifying the three Gospel texts which they had accepted. Francis was not given to this sort of thing, and it took him some time to write down a very short application of the Gospel to a life of poverty, work and prayer.

That, however, was not enough. If there was going to be a written document, then it must be one accepted under obedience to the Holy Father. There was at that time no Church regulation about this, the Fourth Lateran Council in 1215 made that stipulation, but in his high regard for holy Mother Church this seemed to Francis the only right way to proceed. So, with his friars, twelve of them all together, he set off on foot for Rome, simple, poor, unknown, with no authority or credits from anyone. Perhaps he knew that his friend, the Bishop of Assisi, was in Rome at that time, but, in any case, he met him there and was introduced to a saintly Benedictine Cardinal, John of St. Paul, who arranged an audience with Pope Innocent III.

This was a great reforming Pope, a skilled lawyer and diplomat, who ruled with a strong arm. At first he was cool with this tramp from the hill country and dismissed him; But that night he had a dream that seemed to imply that this little poor man was propping up the great Lateran Basilica which was in danger of falling. It made the Pope think, so that the next time when Francis presented his parchment to him, he was mildly favourable; indeed, he was impressed.

But Francis was a spiritual idealist and Innocent III was a spiritual man of great experience and common sense and he had his reservations.

"What you ask," he said, "is a wonderful ideal, but unrealistic. Such extreme poverty as you suggest goes beyond the power of human strength; besides, we must think of those who will come afterwards, lest this way prove too hard for them . . . We will give our approval to your way of life, and give you authority to go and preach penance to all."

The Pope saw to it that they were given the tonsure, which made them clerics, but no formal approval was given in writing, and the document which Francis presented has never been found.

In 1218 Francis was back in Rome St. Dominic was there at that time, and had accepted the Rule of St. Augustine for his friars. Cardinal Hugolino tried to prevail on Francis to do something similar, but he was adamant against it: "Brothers, brothers, the Lord has called me by the way of humility and He has shown me the way of simplicity, and I do not want you to speak to me of any other Rule, neither that of St. Augustine nor of St. Benedict nor of St. Bernard. The Lord told me that He wished me to be a new fool in the world, and that He did not want to lead us by any other way than by that wisdom; for by your learning and your wisdom God will confound you."

A year later Francis set out for the near East, and on his return he settled at Our Lady of the Angels and started to revise his Rule for presentation to the chapter in 1221. Cardinal Hugolino had his say also, not much to Francis' satisfaction. This Rule was never approved, and no one knows what happened to it.

Francis was in ill health and had given up leading the Order, and this office was now in the hands of Friar Elias. About 1223 the Cardinal was again in consultation over the Rule, and Francis went to Fonte Colombo to compose it. It was handed to Elias, who rather carelessly lost it! It seems that the Saint then went to Rome and had further consultations with the Cardinal and Pope Honorius, according to whose advices he had to modify what he had re-written. It seems to be a compromise arranged among the three of them, and it was confirmed by the Pope in 1223 and is the Rule as accepted by all the friars. "This is the Rule of the life of the Friars Minor, namely to observe the Gospel of Our Lord Jesus Christ by living in obedience to Pope Honorius and his canonically elected successors, and to the Roman Catholic Church. All friars must obey Friar Francis and his successors."

The spirit of the Rule is summed up in the words of St. Francis: "The good Friar Minor must love poverty like Brother Bernard, and prayer like Brother Rufino, who prayed even while he slept; he must also lose himself in God like Brother Giles; and be courteous like Brother Angelo and be as patient as Brother Juniper, that perfect imitation of Christ crucified; he must possess the purity and innocence of Brother Leo, the distinction and good sense of Brother Masseo, and finally resemble for charity and detachment from the world of Brother Lucidus, who never stayed more than a month in the same place on the pretext that we have no permanent dwelling place here below."

A PATTERN OF LIFE

We are all aware that there are two kinds of clergy, Secular and Regular. The latter are so called because they follow a Rule - regula in Latin. Such priests and Brothers, and, indeed nuns and Sisters, belong to Religious Orders and in their religious life

40

and work they do not exactly follow their own inclinations, but they observe the Rule under which they have willingly enrolled themselves. It is a sort of pattern of life.

Perhaps you have never adverted to it, but the life of every person who is not just a tramp or a layabout falls into a set pattern. The day is mapped out according to work and leisure. Medically we are encouraged to set ourselves such a patterned existence, so that the body functions according to a healthy rythm. When this is disturbed we can become ill. We all know people, who when they have retired, found themselves unable easily to adapt to a different rythm than that to which they had been accustomed, so that, as we say, they "went to pieces."

What is important for our physical and psychological well-being is equally as important for our spiritual life. Yet how infrequently we think of it! Are you following a rule of some kind, or are you just floundering along? To protect us the Church gives us a very general minimum regulation that we should take part in Mass on Sundays, should say our morning and evening prayers and grace at meals and frequent the sacraments. However, by following a Rule we mean a little more than that. We mean a closer dedication and scheduling of the day in such a way that we allow nothing to impede our movement towards God. Many saintly founders, St. Francis among them, have left such Rules for people living in the world. Even these patterns of life, however, leave much to the initiative of the individual.

Actually it is up to each one to devise his own pattern of spirituality, which will have to telescope into his material pattern of existence. We are composed of body and soul and both must march together. Our daily actions, work, play, sleep, are all

41

to be spiritualised according to the pattern we set our-selves. Since this is meant to become a habit, it is right that children should be given this spiritual regularity, so that it grows with them and can be developed later. A healthy soul in a healthy body is the old adage and this can only be done with regularity. No one should ever be "at a loose end" spiritually, and we are all different.

St. Francis found that he had to temper his own high spiritual ideals to the capabilities of his friars and according to the advices of the Church; his striv-ings and disappointments in regard to his Rule will proportionately appear also in our lives if we fail to appreciate different outlooks and persons. A life pat-tern of one person, even with the same Rule, may not necessarily be that of another. Cardinal Newman has aptly expressed it: "There is no rule about what is happy and good; what suits one would not suit another. And the ways by which perfection is reached vary very much; the medicines necessary for our souls are very different from each other. Thus God leads us by strange ways; we know He wills our happiness, but we neither know what our happiness is, nor the way. We are blind; left to ourselves we should take the wrong way; we must leave it to Him. Let us put ourse-lves into his hands, and not be startled though He leads us by a strange way, a *mirabilis via,* as the Church speaks. Let us be sure He will lead us right, and that He will bring us to that which is, not indeed what *we* think best, nor what is best for another, but what is best for us."

Blessed Be Thou My Lord

For Those Who Patiently Bear Infirmity And Tribulation

THE FIRST FRANCISCAN NUN

March 27th 1211 was Palm Sunday. And a very special Palm Sunday it turned out to be at Assisi. The church of St. Rufino was full of people, ready for the procession and distribution of palms and for the Mass celebrated by the Bishop. The blessed palms were, according to the liturgical custom of that time, handed out by him at the altar rail. After the readings, responses and prayers the people approached, and, kneeling, accepted the palm from the Bishop's hand, kissing both. Last of all came the girls. One girl, however, did not stir from her place in the congregation. She was of a well known family in the town, and so the Bishop noted her absence. He waited at the gates of the sanctuary and looked straight down at her. Clare of Offreduzzo had her eyes cast down and she still did not move. Then, to the wonder of the congregation, Bishop Guido left his place, came up the aisle to Clare, presented her with the palm frond and blessed her. No one could remember such a thing ever happening before, what could it mean? What thoughts, indeed, were occupying the girl so deeply?

Francis was not unknown to Clare. For some time she had been listening to him preaching and she was inspired by his words and by his way of life. He was 30; she was now 18, and had so come to the age of a certain independence. There was much opposition in her household, but she felt God was calling her. Now was her moment of decision. She knew Francis was waiting for her.

During the silence of that Palm Sunday night, while all were sleeping in their beds, Clare, still in her festal dress, quietly left her splendid home; outside she was joined by her faithful friend, Pacifica di Guel-fuccio, and together they took the road down the valley to the friars' huts at Our Lady of the Angels. Brothers Bernard and Philip were there to meet her with lighted torches, and bidding goodbye to Pacifica, they escorted her to Francis, who was waiting with the friars inside the little chapel.

As they chanted the office for the occasion, the refined and delicate Clare put off her shoes and came forward in her bare feet to the sanctuary. Francis knew the rite of acceptance, and placed a rough, coarse habit over her head and tied it with a rope girdle after the fashion of the friars. He then took a knife and cut away her golden hair, which fell to the floor around her. In its place he put a coarse little hood. All then joined in the chanting of the night office until it was finished. Now Francis found himself face to face with a problem! He had never envisaged girls or ladies joining his company, and he had made no provision for them. So, for the time being, he took Clare to the local Benedictine nunnery until he could decide what to do.

He naturally thought of the church on the hillside, St. Damian's, the one he had repaired and where was the Crucifix that had spoken to him. There was a little house, too, and that could be put in order, and he got the friars to work hard at this. In the months that passed, and in spite of the upset in the family, Clare's younger sister, Agnes, came and joined her, and so did some other girls from the town. Eventually all was ready and Francis took them away and installed them at St. Damian's. Clare was most reluctant to accept the title of Abbess, but acceded to the wish of St. Francis, and till her death she remained in charge without a written Rule, but under the personal direction of the Saint himself. Soon girls from the finest families in Assisi were casting aside the spirit of the world and knocking for admittance at St. Damian's. It was the first monastery of the Poor Ladies, or, as they came to be known, the "Poor Clares."

Poverty became their sole inheritance. In every season of the year they went barefooted with a rough cassock style dress. One large room, cold and bare, served them, and each bed was formed of twigs with a log of wood for a pillow and patched bits of cloth for sheets. Food was what they begged from passers-by, or what the friars brought; otherwise they willingly fasted. It was this primacy of poverty that they regarded as their unique privilege - poverty prayer and penance.

There are three groups of Poor Clares. First, those using the strict Rule of St. Clare herself, second, those following a mitigated Rule allowed by Pope Urban IV, whence they are known as Urbanists, and third, those living according to the reformed Rule of St. Colette, who are known as Colettines. The Urbanists, who were established in England until the Reformation, have never returned. The others now have monasteries here, most being Colletines. Besides these Franciscan Nuns, there are also Franciscan Sisters who follow adaptations of the Rule of the Third Order, as it used to be called, now known as the Secular Franciscan Order. There are about eighteen such Orders working in the British Isles, eight of which were founded here.

Clare di Offreduzzo had a strong personality and knew her rights. On the other hand she had no exaggerated sense of importance of herself and she realized her proper place in society and in the Church. She never suffered from an induced inferiority complex because God had created here woman and not a man; she did not arrogate to herself or to her Ladies works and offices that were not meant for them. She followed the Gospel and Tradition in all simplicity under the authority of the Church. It never occurred to her, to tell Christ what he should have done, might have done, ought to have done, or could have done. Because of her humble obedience and her acceptance of her place as a woman in God's plan of creation, redemption and providence she exercised a great influence over her contemporaries and on the centuries since. Her power is still strong and her ideals will last for centuries yet to come, when all the modern feminine aggressiveness will have faded into the pages of history.

There is an enormous amount of good done unobtrusively by enclosed Religious in prayer, work and penance. The world of grace is spread and intensified all around us by these people. They are the power houses of the Church. The very fact that they live in silent meditation, in prayer and fasting, working for a simple living, close to God, when all the world about them is embroiled in noise, shouting for rights, calling for changes, up-datings and re-alignings, conferencings, interminable argy-bargy and meetings - this very fact makes many people look upon them as rather usless and doing nothing. The "heresy of activism" cannot understand the silent, dedicated, victim soul.

Perhaps we need to assimilate a lot more the spirit of St. Clare, to realize that it is not always the people who create most fuss and objective concern who are doing the most work; that it is not necessary to live in a constant whirl of human endeavour - even seemingly religious - to achieve the deepest spiritual experience of benefit. We should examine our lives in this regard, and perhaps in many cases simplify them and march quietly and confidently with our hands in the hands of God. Those girls or young women who might wish to walk closer along the way of Franciscan perfection would always be welcome to enquire at any Poor Clare monastery.

Dal Cantico delle Creature

THE PERPLEXED SAINT

In 1214 a certain Count Orlando gave Francis and his brethren the Mount of Alverna as a place of prayer and retreat. To Francis, who saw the finger of God in everything, this caused a certain uneasiness; was it perhaps a sign that he should cease going about and preaching in towns, but should rather dedicate himself to a life of solitude, prayer and penance? Throughout his life he relied very much on prudent advice and seldom made a decision on his own. He tells us "From the beginning of my conversion the Lord put his word in the mouth of the Bishop of Assisi, so that he gave me good advice and fortified me in the service of Christ."

His present evangelical mode of life stemmed from February 1208, when he had heard Mass at Our Lady of the Angels and had heard the words of the Gospel: "Go rather to the lost sheep of the House of Israel, and preach as you go, telling them that the Kingdom of Heaven is at hand ... Give as you have received the gift, without payment; do not provide gold or silver or copper to fill your purses, nor a wallet for the journey, no second coat, no spare shoes or staff. In whatever city or village you enter, find who is worthy there, and entering in let your salutation be: 'Peace be with you.' (Matt. 10.6-12). It was with this advice that he launched his mission onto the world.

When later he went with eleven companions to Rome, Cardinal Colonna received them most graciously but advised that they should join an existing religious Order or become hermits. The latter would have suited Francis, but he now had followers to think of who looked to him for organization and guidance. The Pope was perhaps more understanding, who recommended hesitancy and prayer. It was with this admonition ringing in their ears that they returned to Assisi.

49

In 1221, when Francis resigned as General of the Order, he still was perplexed about his mission in life. He called those of his brethren who were near him, and asked: "What do ye counsel, Brethren, what do ye commend? Shall I devote myself unto prayer, or shall I go about preaching? Of a truth, I that am little and simple and uncultured in speech have received more grace of prayer than of speaking. Now in prayer there seemeth to be the gain and heaping up of graces; in preaching a certain giving out of gifts received from heaven: in prayer, again, a cleansing of the inward feelings, and an union with the one, true and highest God together with a strengthening of virtue; in preaching the spiritual feet wax dusty and many things distract a man and discipline is relaxed: finally, in prayer we speak with God and hear Him, and live as it were the life of angels; in preaching we must practise much condescension towards men, and, living among them as fellow men, must think, say, see and hear such things as pertain unto men. Yet, one thing is there to set against these, which in God's sight would seem to weigh more than they all; the fact that the only begotten Son of God, who is the highest wisdom, left his Father's bosom for the salvation of souls, that instructing the world by his example, He might preach the word of salvation to men ... Forasmuch as we ought to do all things after the pattern of those things that were shown us in Him as on the lofty mount, it seems to me that it might be more acceptable to God, that laying aside leisure, I should go forth unto the work." St. Bonaventure tells us: " ... he would enquire of wise and simple, of perfect and imperfect, of young and old in what way he might with most holiness attain to the summit of perfection."

Then one day Francis called Friar Masseo to him and told him: "Go to Sister Clare and bid her from me that she and some of the most spiritual of her companions pray devoutly to God, that He may be pleased to reveal to me which is the more excellent way: whether to give myself up to preaching or wholly to prayer. Then go to Friar Sylvester and bid him do the like." So off went Masseo to Clare at St. Damian's, informed her of the message, and while she and her nuns set to prayer, he went off on the longer journey to Friar Sylvester. This friar was a priest who had taken to living as a hermit away up on the hillside of Mount Subasio, at a gorge now known as the Carcere. Masseo found him, and together they spent a long time in prayer. Sylvester eventually rose and said to him: "Go to Friar Francis and say to him that God has not called him to this state for himself alone, but that he may bring forth fruit of souls, and that many through him may be saved." On the way Masseo called in at St. Clare, and from her received the same answer. When he returned to Our Lady of the Angels, Francis knelt before him and enquired, "What does my Lord Jesus command?" Masseo told him: "Thus to Friar Sylvester and to Sister Clare and her sisterhood hath Christ answered and revealed his will: that you go forth to preach throughout the world, for He hath not chosen thee for thyself alone, but also for the salvation of others."

ACCEPTING ADVICE AND COUNSEL

Change is part of life; stagnation means death. Change for the mere sake of change is a bad thing; change that means betterment and progression is a sensible thing. Everyone sets themselves ideals, in vocation, profession or trade, and this indeed is a necessity. To push ahead with perseverance towards an ideal is a praiseworthy effort; but, on the other hand, to "bash one's head against a stone wall" is hardly commendable! A sensible person appreciates the difference.

In the life of every person God works, not by direct inspiration, but through other people and through circumstances. A young person may set themselves the ideal of joining a Religious Order, and they start their novitiate or trial year. Perhaps they decide for themselves and leave, but they should not give up the ideal; they may fit in some other Order. On the other hand, a person may be told to leave, and this comes much harder. This is an instance where one's own will had to be brought into alignment with the will of God expressed through others. To accept a a change of direction is sensible; not to accept it, is to bash one's head.

Students in higher studies, and craftsmen apprenticed to a trade may well fancy a certain line of study, but progress reports and tutorial advice may suggest a change of emphasis. The young craftsman may fancy himself, say, as a cabinet maker, but advices might bring him to. realize that he would make a far better carpenter and joiner. It is good to be docile and to recognize the finger of God in well given advice and the juxtaposition of events. To be flexible within limits, to be adaptable, is an excellent characteristic. Not to accept our limitations and inabilities is simply to cause trouble; it eventually leads into frustration complexes, nervous upsets, and recriminations against all and sundry.

Body and soul work together, and if we are in a constant state of external agitation and pressure, the soul and our spiritual life will suffer also. The life of St. Francis shows us how flexible he was, how he saw the hand of God in events and advices. His Rule had to be tempered to his followers; the advices from bishops and the Church were not always to his own way of thinking; his own life was decided by Holy

Scripture, by Clare and Friar Sylvester. He accepted all these things and so developed a peace of mind and could praise God always. We should endeavour to do the same. Have great ideals, but realise the difficulties; have one's own opinion, but be willing to accede to the considered opinions of others.

THE SECULAR ORDER OR ST. FRANCIS

As the fame and the ideals of St. Francis became known men and women flocked to enrol under his banner of Gospel observance and poverty of life. This was all very well for those who were uncommitted and free, but there were others who were already bound by obligations to society, in the business world and in the Church. They, too, wished to adopt his way of life, but how they were to do it, wasn't clear.

Francis first became aware of this problem at a little place called Saburniano, where he bade the swallows be silent while he preached, and at Cannara, where the people who could not join his company almost demanded solution to their problem. What should they do? Some, indeed, were prepared to forsake all and to follow him, but the Saint counselled prudence: "Be not in haste to depart, for I will ordain what ye shall do for the health of your souls."

It was about this time that Francis wrote his "Letter to All the Faithful." It was a sort of first draft of the Third Order Rule, and sought to impress upon everyone that necessity of following the Gospel more closely. "The Gospel orders us to love our neighbours as ourself. Let us then do good to our brethren instead of doing evil; if it is our business to judge, let us judge with mercy; if our function is to command, let us exercise our powers with indulgence, considering ourselves as the servants of others; if it be our role to obey, let us do it with humility, unless what is commanded us is a sin; let us practice penance; let us give generously to the poor; and finally, let us be simple, modest and pure rather than prudent and wise according to the flesh."

This letter went out in 1214, and in the years following Francis and Cardinal Hugolino, his great friend, drew up a Rule of Life for all those people who could not become friars or nuns. In the year 1221 Francis preached with marked effect in Poggibonsi, Tuscany. Listening in the crowd was a rich merchant who had been one of Francis' associates in the youthful, frivolous days at Assisi and Perugia. His family was also engaged in the cloth trade, and no doubt, had common interests with the Bernardone family. Luchesio was not only a successful business man but also a politician of some importance, and he was at Poggibonsi with his pretty wife because of political troubles in Siena.

Luchesio and Buonadonna were full of worldly ideas and ambitions and their life was not very edifying. But hearing Francis speak made Luchesio realize that while his life was successful worldly-wise, it was nevertheless being wasted. They talked this over and then resolved to accept the way of life of which Francis had spoken; so they became the first two members of the Third Order, or, as it is now known, the Secular Order of St. Francis. Their fine house was opened up to the sick and the poor, and Luchesio went out through the villages bringing them in, while Buonadonna nursed them and cared for them. When eventually resources ran low, because all their income was at the disposal of the poor and infirm, Luchesio followed the example of St. Francis, and, gentlemen though he was, took the begging bowl and went from door to door.

The Rule of life was simple: "Be good Christians; dress simply and modestly; keep away from dancing and theatres; learn how to conquer yourself; help the poor and the sick; restore anything you have acquired unjustly; make a will and dispose of your effects according to justice, thus avoiding discord, rancour and litigation; keep away from factions and cliques; be reconciled with enemies; do not carry arms unless for the defence of Church or Country; and do not swear oaths unless to maintain peace, to promote the Faith, or in the course of judicial proceedings."

Since Francis' Day this way of life, adapted to times and circumstances, has been followed by countless thousands, noblemen, ecclesiastics, scholars, the poor and insignificant as well as the great. All have found the same source of sanctification in the advice of the Saint of Assisi, and that advice is still as valid and efficacious as it ever was.

WORKING TOGETHER

We live in a 'do-it-yourself' age. Every individual seems to be engaged in doing his or her 'thing.' Doing one's own "thing" no doubt has certain advantages, but there are also decided drawbacks. In unity is strength, and there is little unity when everyone is simply pleasing themselves. Shared responsibility and shared experience lead to a greater and more amicable achievement, and, providing one is not simply just leaning on another, then the society or organization with each contributing his full part, is more competent than the individual.

This is also true spiritually: "Where two or three are gathered together in my name, there am I in the midst of them." Co-operation in the promotion of the works of mercy, charity and prayer has always been part of Catholic Church life; indeed, it is one of the purposes of all Religious Orders, confraternities, pious unions and societies of all kinds. The trend today would seem to be away from this group work, each person having ideas of their own. Everyone appears to want to command, no one to obey; pride of position takes the place of humility; carving a niche for oneself appears more important than serving the group. So, in common with other societies, Third Orders, as they were called, lost much of their force with diminished numbers. One often heard it said that a new era demanded new societies, but even where these have arisen they have not commanded the same following as was given by previous generations to the Church societies of a former time. Perhaps it has something to do with modern lifestyles.

Anyhow, a result of the Second Vatican Council was that all Religious Orders, confraternities and societies of whatever kind re-examined their aims and constitutions - and so did the Franciscan Order. Thus, its ideals, purposes and the particular form of spirituality were reasserted, but methods and policy were up-dated to fit life in the modern world. The "Secular Order of St. Francis" is geared to have a deep impact on the individual and on society.

It involves two aspects: a spiritual and prayer life combined with a simple life-style; then an over-flowing of this spirituality in works of mercy and charity. Love of God and love of one's neighbour is the Gospel command. The golden thread is a progressive reforming of one's life in the Franciscan pattern of simple living, contentment, joy and peace, which leads, as it did with the Saint, to a deep union with God. Days of renewal, retreats, recollection in traditional or more modern forms, recommended reading and the monthly meetings are all conducive to building up this Franciscan personality.

This spiritual bond of the Secular Order places no restraint on individual effort in good works, and no one is pressurised into this or that type of action. Obviously united efforts channelling work into one sphere might often be more productive. The better promotion of charitable works often means sinking one's own 'thing' and proceeding with others in a spirit of humility and obedience to a leader.

Consequently, why not unite in Christ and Francis? Receive added spiritual help and direction by belonging to the Order that he himself established. Follow in the footsteps of B1. Luchesio and B1. Buonadonna in helping one's fellow man. Almost every Franciscan Friary will have a centre of the Secular Order of St. Francis, and it is only a matter of enquiry to find out where these centres are.

Blessed Be Thou My Lord

**For Those Who Pardon
For Love Of Thee.**

NOT FOR OURSELVES ALONE ...
BUT ALSO FOR OTHERS

The salvation of souls was always uppermost in the mind of St. Francis and he declared that nothing was to be preferred to this, because "The Son of God died for them on the Cross." His apostolic zeal made him become a wandering preacher around Italy, into France, Spain, Illeria, Palestine and Egypt; his three Orders were dedicated to this preaching of the Gospel and reformation of life, and the poverty and simplicity of their lives was witness to their mission. Repentence, peace, pardon and joy in the Lord were the key words.

On the 16th of July 1212 the Christians reported a resounding victory over the Moslems at Toulouse, and when news of this percolated to Assisi it set Francis afire with zeal to preach the Gospel to them. Two years later, with Friar Bernard of Quintavalle, he left Italy, traversed Provence and went over the Pyrenees and into Spain. Here he fell violently ill. God stopped him in his steps! Meekly he bowed his head, waited until he became sufficiently well again, and then retraced his steps back to Assisi.

The friars were accustomed to assemble at St. Mary of the Angels for a Pentecostal Chapter, and in 1217 Francis addressed them with his usual simplicity and unfolded before them a vast design of evangelization. "Go two and two with humility and trust in God. As you proclaim peace with your lips, have it in your own hearts ... In a meek and pleasant manner call all to repentance, to pardon, to a love of God and one's neighbour. Remember that we are destined for the salvation of souls, for the comfort of those who mourn, and to recall to the ways of justice and truth all those who have erred." He appointed Ministers

Provincial, and assigned Friar Elias of Assisi to that mission which he himself most favoured, Syria and the Near East.

Two years later in 1219 at a similar Pentecostal assembly, Cardinal Hugolino, then 80 years old, soon to be Pope as Gregory IX, clad in the grey habit of the Brethren, rode on his horse among them and declared with astonishment: "Truly this is a grand field of the Knights of God!" Francis directed his friars into the various mission areas. "The King of Verses" went to Western France, Friar John Bonelli of Florence to Provence, Friar Christopher of Romagna to Aquitaine, John Parenti to Spain, John of Penna to Germany, Agnellus of Pisa to England; others were sent to Hungary and into Tunisia. Francis then turned to a group of Umbrian friars and said to them: "My sons, God has commanded me to send you among the Saracens of Morocco to preach openly the Faith of Christ. Prepare to fulfil this wish of Our Saviour." "We are ready," they answered, and as the assembly dispersed five friars set out for Morocco, Berard, who spoke Arabic fluently, Peter, Otto, Accurso and Adjuto. On the way they stopped at an Augustinian priory at Coimbra, where they greatly impressed a canon named Ferdinand. In Africa they very soon fell, martyrs, under the scimitars of the Sultan's men. Their bodies were brought back by merchants to Coimbra, and so inspired by their zeal and fortitude was the canon Ferdinand, that he transferred from the Augustinians to the new Franciscan Order, taking the name Anthony - Anthony of Padua to the whole world, but still Anthony of Lisbon to the Portugese.

Meanwhile, Francis himself undertook to go to the Holy Land where the Fifth Crusade was in progress. On the 24th June he left Ancona with twelve friars. They touched at Candia, then Cyprus, and visited Friar Elias at Acra who had been working there for two years with great missionary success. So they arrived at Damietta, where the Christian army was getting ready to engage the Moslems. Francis advised against this. His advice was not accepted, and the whole affair ended in a dreadful fiasco and defeat for the Christians. Undeterred by this and by the fact that the Sultan, Melek-el-Kamel, had placed a price on the head of any Christian, Francis felt that he must go and place the teachings of Christ before the Sultan. With Friar Illuminato he approached the Egyptian encampment, and shouted to the soldiers the only word he knew, "Sultan, Sultan!" He got rough treatment, but they understood what he wanted and a message was sent to Malek. In due course the two Italians appeared before the great man who was most surprised to find that they had not come seeking privileges of some sort. He listened respectfully as they talked about Christ and the Church, he admired their courage, and then he gave them gifts and told them to be off. It was all rather disappointing, but there was a compensation when, back at the Christian camp, Francis met Friar Elias who had come especially to meet him, and received to the Order a famous German preacher, Caesar of Spires.

In his Rule St. Francis especially recommended the foreign missions: "Whoever of the friars by divine inspiration desires to go among the Saracens and other infidels, shall ask leave from his Minister Provincial. The Minster shall grant permission to none save those whom they consider capable."

YOUR MISSIONARY OUTLOOK

As Catholics we are apt to become very self-satisfied with ourselves and our religious environment. We have the Faith, and we are grateful for that;

we practice our religious duties, we educate our children in the Faith of their Fathers, we contribute to Church support, and, all in all, we are fairly good Catholics.

Of course, that is all very well, but does it not seem that something is lacking? Are we not falling short on an essential element? Remember what St. Clare advised St. Francis, "We are sent not to save our own souls only, but also the souls of others." The injunction given by Our Lord "Going, therefore, teach ye all nations," we consider as given to the Apostles, the first bishops, and that it therefore applies to the hierarchy of the Church. Essentially this is so, but surely it is an order given also to every Catholic? Are you involved in "teaching all nations" equally as much as the priests, brothers and sisters who are working foreign parts?

Your involvement is different, but equally important. In these days many lay people are becoming more conscious of their responsibilities, and many professional people, craftsmen - doctors, nurses, carpenters, bricklayers, etc. are giving some years of their lives to work in a particular mission. Perhaps that is not within everybody's scope, but there are other ways.

There is a rather false impression creeping in that primitive peoples are best left alone; that if we do anything, we should simply alleviate their material conditions. This is to place secondary things first. We are there to preach the Gospel: "Seek ye first the Kingdom of Heaven, and all these other things will be added to you." In this way both the spiritual and the material advance together. In St. Francis' ideal there was no consideration at all of the material; the mission to Morocco and the East was one simply of conversion to Christ. When later friars under John of

Monte Corvino traversed Central Asia to Pekin and established there a Catholic hierarchy in the fifteenth century, it was a truly spiritual venture.

In what way, then, are you personally involved in this great missionary enterprise of the Church? Is it just to flip a few coins onto a plate a few times a year? That's not doing much! There are some few persons who are actively involved in prayer and support by affiliation to missionary Orders. The mass of Catholics, though, are still on the outside looking in. Dioceses are nowadays sending volunteer secular priests into various mission fields, which the diocese "adopts." This has lead also to parishes adopting a particular mission station, or, "twinning", as they call it. Thus spiritual and material help is provided, not in an haphazard way, but on a regular basis.

If up to now you have not been doing anything in particular, if your parish has not twinned with some mission, if your Catholic friends, societies, clubs, etc. have not developed a mission-conscious outlook, perhaps you are the person to suggest and start such a venture. Why not now? Why wait for tomorrow?

LOYALTY TO THE CHURCH

In Italy at the time of St. Francis there was a certain indifference to religion, a certain coolness between the clergy and the people. Because of the various standards of living among the different classes of society, and the injustice that followed from this, various reforming groups had arisen in Italy and France. Many of these groups, however, went to extremes, imagining that they could attain their aims by attacking the Church: thus they fell into heresy. This in turn led to the Church taking a very serious and perhaps suspicious outlook on anyone attempting to bring about reforms.

Pope Innocent III was very conscious of all this, and was most solicitous that due reform be set in motion in the Church and in society, and for this purpose he convened the Great Council of the Lateran, in 1215. Francis was in Rome at that time and shared the general enthusiasm. He felt himself called to take a part in this work, adopting as his own that sign of predeliction, the Tau Cross, mentioned by the Pope quoting the Prophet Ezekiel. Innocent had mentioned three types of chosen men: those who rallied to the Crusade which he called for, those, who unable to do this, occupied themselves combatting heresy, and those who tried hard to reform their own lives and those of their fellows.

Unlike the many heretical groups, whose idea of reform was to change the Church, Francis threw his whole effort into support for the Church of God; the reform first of one's own life, and from the example thus given the consequent reform of others.

A famous bishop of those times, Jacques de Vitry tells us what he admired in Umbria one year after the Council of the Lateran: "What I saw, which was consoling, was the large number of men and women who had renounced their wealth and had quitted the world for the love of Christ. These men who bore the name of Friars Minor are held by the Pope and the Cardinals in the highest esteem . . . Thanks be to God, they have already had important success and made numerous conquests, for they are adepts at recruiting others and their hearers multiply of themselves.

As to their manner of life, it is that of the Primitive Church, where, as the Scripture says, the multitude of believers had but one heart and one soul. By day they are found in the towns and villages preaching or at work; at night they return to their hermitages where they give themselves in solitude to prayer."

At the chapter of Mats St. Francis in the first place pledged his friars to obey the Church and to pray for Christendom. "Know ye, brethren, that the fruit of souls is most pleasing to God, and it can be better gained by peace with the clergy than by strife with them." His attitude towards the Church and the clergy is obvious from his life and sayings: "Let all brethren be Catholics and live and speak as such . . . And let us hold all the clergy and all Religious Lords in those things which concern the salvation of the soul . . . Let us revere their Order, office and administration in the Lord."

"Blessed is the servant who puts trust in the clergy who live uprightly according to the form of the Holy Roman Church, and woe to those who depise them; for though they be sinners no man ought to judge them, for that the Lord Himself alone reserves them for Himself to judge. For by how much greater than all others is their ministry of the Body and Blood of Our Lord Jesus Christ which they receive and alone minister to others, by so much greater is the sin of those who sin against them that of those who sin against any other man in this world."

He said on one occasion: "If I chanced to meet at the same time any saint coming from heaven and any poor priest, I would do honour to the presbyter first, and would sooner go to kiss his hands, and I would say to the other, 'Oh, wait for me St. Laurence, for the hands of this man handle the Word of Life, and possess that which is more than human.'" "When he had anything particular to say to them, he called the clergy aside lest lay people should hear them being reproved. He showed a very marked respect and deference to prelates, and would never preach to the people until he had the required authority.

"The Church of Rome," he says, "is the Mother of all the Churches and the sovereign head of all religious Orders. I shall always have recourse to her and recommend my brethren to her . . . Our Holy Mother the Church will zealously protect the glory of our poverty. She will not allow the precious virtue of humility to be obscured by the clouds of pride; by severely punishing all who create discord among us, she will strenghten the bond of peace and charity, so that nothing will be able to break it. Under her eye evangelical observance will flourish in its primitive beauty; for she will never allow these devout usages which diffuse the sweet and refreshing odour of Christ around us, to be neglected even for a time. Let my children, then, be grateful to their Mother for the favours and help they receive from her; let them remain prostrate at her feet with profound reverence, and be always inviolably attached to her."

CO-OPERATION WITH THE CHURCH

In other times and in different places church and parish management has varied. It still varies quite a bit from country to country. At present we are in a state of progressive change as a result of the Vatican Council II, and on both sides there are, as usual, the extremities; the traditionalists, who see no reason for change at all, and the modernists who want to over-turn everything. This leads to a great lot of criticism, which does not help constructive change.

We would do well to remember that far more than in the time of St. Francis the Church today is under constant attack. Indeed, the very idea of God is openly contested. We need to understand more than ever "Ubi Petrus, ibi Ecclesia" - "Where Peter is, there is the Church," and stand in close allegiance to the Vicar of Christ, the Rock on which the Church is founded. In the spirit of St. Francis we should be very slow to lend an ear to criticisms of the clergy, the Church and the Holy Father.

Whatever we think of collegiality, democratis-tion, laity involvement, up-dating and all that sort of thing, the fact is that the priest is still the ordained leader in the Church community. He is not answera-ble to the people but to his bishop, and finally to God Himself; he has his authority, not from election by the people, but from the divine magisterium of the Church. It may be that his own spiritual life may not be as dedicated as that of some of the people he serves, but because of this the laity should not easily take and propagate scandal. To someone who comp-lained to him about a certain priest, St. Francis answered: "The hands of this priest may be such as you say; I know nothing about it, but even if they be so they cannot change the virtue of the Sacraments. By those hands God bestows on his people a mul-titude of graces; I kiss those hands in honour of the benefits they dispense and of Him whose instruments they are."

Our attitude to the Holy Church should be similar. It is the voice of God upon earth, and there is no other, but it speaks through weak, human instruments. We owe it and its ministers our whole-hearted and unwavering loyalty in the great effort of propagating the Gospel in which we, each in his own way, are all partners. Are we doing this? Are we teaching our children to do it?

Blessed Be Thou My Lord

For Brother Fire, By Whom Thou Dost Illumine The Night.

GRECCIO AND THE CRIB

When he was in the Holy Land there was one place that appears to have deeply impressed Francis and that was Bethlehem. The thought of the Son of God born there in poverty of the Virgin Mary was uppermost in his mind when he returned to Italy, and his regard for the feast of Christmas became very deep and personal, with an increased devotion to the Infancy of Christ.

He was wont to call Christmas "The Feast of Feasts," and on that day every creature of God should partake in the joy of mankind. "If I can have speech of the Emperor to entreat and persuade him, I will ask that for the love of God and of me he will make a special law that no one should take or kill our sisters, the larks, nor do them any harm; and likewise that all the magistrates of cities and lords of fortresses and villages should be bound every year on Christmas Day to compel men to throw out corn and other grain on the roads outside the cities and fortresses, that our sisters the larks, and other birds too, may have somewhat to eat on the day of so great a festival; and that for reverence to the Son of God, whom, as on that night the most blessed Virgin Mary laid in a manger between the ox and the ass, everyone who has an ox and an ass should be bound that night to provide them abundantly with good fodder; and likewise that on that day all the poor should be satisfied by the rich with good food."

One year when Christmas fell on a Friday Friar Morico thought it only right to maintain the abstinence from flesh meat customary on that day. But Francis reproved him: "What! it would indeed be a real sin to think of a Friday on a great Feast like this;

69

the very walls themselves would have the right to eat meat today, and, if that is impossible, one might at least rub them down with fat so that they eat meat in their fashion."

After his visit to Rome in 1223, where he had had the Rule approved by the Holy Father, though somewhat disappointed he nevertheless felt a great peace of soul, he retired to the district of Fonte Colombo where he always experienced a great nearness to God. He liked this place for its quietness and seclusion. Also he had a good friend here, John of Velita, the knight who owned the property. It was a few weeks before Christmas and Francis suggested to him that he had thought of a new way to celebrate the feast. He had spoken of this previously to Pope Honorius, for he would not act without permission from the Church, and the Pope had agreed. "Listen, John, this coming Christmas Eve I would like to portray the birth of Christ in the manger in a way that has not been done before. Find a suitable cave among the trees; put a manger in there, set it up with straw and bring in an ox and an ass."

By Christmas Eve John of Velita had everything ready; the friars came from various hermitages, the people from the surrounding districts came through the night carrying torches and lighted candles. Then the priest to say the Mass arrived with Francis as his assistant, vested in the dalmatic which was his as a deacon. With hymns and chants that re-echoed through the keen midnight air the Mass began and went forward; Francis chanted the Gospel in a loud, clear voice, and then preached to the congregation on the mystery of Bethlehem and the poverty and love of the divine Child. It is said that in this first Christmas Crib the Child Jesus appeared lying in the manger and smiled up at Francis as he knelt before Him.

EXTERNAL STIMULI

The crib is nowadays part of the Christmas scene. Even most non-Catholics, who have overcome their aversion to statues, now set up a crib in their churches. Another similar para-liturgical rite of more recent vintage is the Advent wreath and the Advent Candles, preparing us step by step for the great feast. In some churches an Easter Sepulchre or Easter Garden is set up at that time to commemorate the risen Christ. The Palm Sunday procession is another well known example.

We are constituted of body and soul, the physical and the spiritual. Nothing is in the mind that is not first in the senses, and the senses are the windows of the soul. Our approach to spiritual appreciation and progress is often through the sensory perceptions, and this is a fact that is generally recognised. How odd, then, if such were not to be used in our relationship with God. So it is that the Catholic Church is very concerned to impress upon us the truths of Faith and the way of the Gospel through her liturgical rites, her para-liturgical observances as mentioned above, through the use of colour, movement, singing, statues and other such objects.

But this necessity for external stimulus surely does not just begin and end in church. The home, likewise, should be a centre of such activity. The feasts of the church year and the doctrine we believe should be impressed on us by external manifestations in the family circle: the crib at Christmas, for instance, palm in a conspicuous place during Holy Week, a small shrine and light before a picture of the Sacred Heart of Jesus or before a statue of Our Lady, before which we would usually say our night prayers. No person is so spiritually advanced that he doesn't need some of these external stimuli.

What about your home? How do you rate in this regard? Are you starving your soul, and shutting the windows on it? Is your home recognisable as a Catholic one with a picture of Our Lord or Our Lady or some saint, or perhaps with a small statue in an obvious position - or are you ashamed to be known for what you are? Is your home no different to the visitor from the home of the modern pagan up the street? We should be proud to be Catholics and followers of Christ. We should stand up and be counted, make ourselves known and give signs of the convictions that we hold. This external stimuli attracts others, thought is encouraged, questions are asked, and thus other people are gradually brought to know Christ and his Church.

THE SERAPH OF ALVERNA

In 1224 St. Francis and Friar Elias were together preaching in the cities of Umbria. One night, when they were staying near Foligno, Elias had a vision of a priestly old man who said to him: "Arise, Brother, and announce to Bro. Francis that eighteen years have now passed since he renounced the world and gave himself wholly to Our Lord. Say also to him that there remain yet but two years before that God shall call him to Himself."

They then returned to the brethren at Our Lady of the Angels, where in June Francis attended what was to be his last chapter of friars. Afterwards he began to think of his annual vigil and fast, his particular "Lent", as he called it, covering the Feast of St. Michael, to whom he always had a great devotion. Where would he go for solitude and prayer, which he felt was more necessary now than ever? He had a few favourite places, Lake Trasimene, Fonte Colombo, the Carcere, but it was not these that was in his mind now, for he remembered La Verna, a wild and secluded mountain, 4,000 feet high and about forty miles from Assisi. In the Spring of 1214, it had been allocated for his use and that of his friars by Count Orlando of Chiusi. Now is was to become the scene of a stupendous mystical event the like of which the Church had never seen.

Francis therefore, left Assisi with the three companions, Friars Leo, Angelo and Rufino, accompanied also by Sylvester, the priest, and by Illuminato and Masseo. When they arrived they were please to know that the Count had expected them and was there to greet them: "My very dear Brothers, it is not my intention that you should want for anything on this mountain and so be distracted from your spiritual

73

duties; I bid you, therefore, once and for all, freely to come to me for anything you need, and be assured that if you act otherwise, I shall not take it in good part."

They set to work to construct themselves little shelters near to the tiny chapel, also called Our Lady of the Angels. When all was ready Francis spoke to them and admonished them on several things, telling them: "Since I feel that I draw near to death, I wish to be alone and to find refuge with God and to bewail my sins. Brother Leo shall bring me a little bread and water, and do you not allow that any who are of the world to come near me."

At the solitude of his hut Francis prayed and fasted for his Order which he seemed to see passing from his own high ideals; he lamented his own sins and the sins of the world; he went into deep contemplation of the Passion of Our Lord, of his intense love for mankind that made Him endure so much suffering that the sins of the world might be taken away. He gazed on the great rocks and the chasms about him, and it seemed to him that all this must have come about when the Saviour was crucified "The rocks were split and the veil of the temple was rent in twain." He moved closer to their embrace until they enfolded him in their fastness and gave him refuge and isolation on a stern rocky ledge. Here he physically suffered greatly and the devil attacked him to try to drive him to despair, but in the midst of his penances and prayer angels came and strengthened him. It was a period of purification before the great gift.

On the eve of the Feast of the Holy Cross, Francis, deeply engrossed in prayer, besought God: "My Lord Jesus Christ, I beg two graces of Thee before I die: to experience myself, as far as possible, the sufferings of thy cruel Passion, and to have for Thee that very love which caused Thee to sacrifice Thyself for us." About one hour before sunrise, as St. Bonaventure narrates: "Suddenly from the height of heaven a Seraph, having six wings of flame, swept down towards him. It appeared in the image of a man hanging on a cross. Two wings at the head, two others served for flight, and the last two covered the body. It was Christ Himself, who, in order to manifest Himself to the blessed one, appeared in this guise. It rested on the living wall of stone, fixed Francis with its gaze, then left him, having imprinted on his flesh the sacred Stigmata of the Crucifixion. From this moment, · indeed, Francis was marked with the wounds of the divine Redeemer. His feet, his hands, seemed pierced with nails of which the round black heads appeared in the palms of the hands and on the feet, the points thrust through the flesh bent back. And there, too, on the right side, was a wound as though made by a lance, from which the blood frequently oozed, even through his shirt and tunic."

His first inclination was to hide this great favour, but he came to the correct conclusion that it would be impossible. Returning to the brethren, he consulted them as to whether extraordinary graces should be kept secret or ought to be revealed.

It was Friar Illuminato who answered: "Brother Francis, I think that thou mayest be wrong in keeping to thyself what God intended for the edification of all." So Francis made known to the brethren how Christ had visited him on the rock and what had happened to him, but he was always very careful to hide his wounds from the general public. After his death the five Wounds were observed on his body by many reliable witnesses as well as the friars, and among Franciscans the day of the Stigmata, September 14th is now observed as a liturgical feast.

THE WOUNDS IMPRESSED ON US

This was an extraordinary gift bestowed upon St. Francis, but it brought with it pain entailed in those same wounds. We somethimes forget that. We read about people especially dedicated to God, those who dedicatetheir entire life to works of charity and mercy and we admire the wonderful gifts they have, a loving and sympathetic nature, a sort of charisma that brings the best out of others, a flair for organization and administrative ability; but seldom do we consider the actual pain with which these people have to live, their continual anxious concern for projects undertaken, their mental anguish when friends and helpers let them down with a bump, the actual physical suffering which is sometimes part of their life. Such persons walk confidently with their hand in the hand of Our Saviour, and so a share of his Wounds becomes theirs. It is not external and observable as was the Stigmata of St. Francis, but the impression is there nevertheless.

To some degree this can be said of every person who walks with Christ. There were those great saints, strong souls, who actually prayed for suffering that they might thus enter more deeply into his redemptive work. The most of us can hardly aspire to that strength, but in the ordinary course of events we will receive that impression of the Wounds that God sees good for us. We shall all have to suffer something; most of us are gravely ill at some time in our lives, and as death approaches, whether we are young or old, some pain is inevitable. This is our share of the Stigmata, and as St. Francis willingly accepted the pain,

76

so we ought to follow him in accepting with resignation to the Divine Will whatever may come upon us. Perhaps Cardinal Newman summed it all up for us in his very human prayer: "O my dear Lord, though I am so very weak that I am not fit to ask Thee for suffering as a gift, and have not strength to do so, at least I will beg of Thee grace to meet suffering well, when Thou in thy love and wisdom dost bring it upon me. Let me bear pain, reproach, disappointment, slander, anxiety, suspense, as Thou wouldst have me, O my Jesus, and as Thou by thy own suffering has taught me, when it comes. And I promise, too, with thy grace, that I will never set myself up, never seek pre-eminence, never court any great thing of the world, never prefer myself to others. I wish to bear insult meekly, and to return good for evil. I wish to humble myself in all things, and to be silent when I am ill-used, and to be patient when sorrow or pain is prolonged, and all for the love of Thee and thy Cross, knowing that in this way I shall gain the promise of this life and of the next."

WELCOME SISTER DEATH

During the late Summer of 1226 Francis of Assisi was not at his home town. He had been ill for a very long time and getting progressively worse, and, in compliance with Friar Elias' wish, he had gone to Siena to be under the care of the Pope's physician. The medical care, however, did him no good, and he expressed a desire to be back in Assisi. In order to avoid Perugia, which was again at enmity with Assisi, he was brought back by the rough mountain tracks, through Borgo San Sepulchro, Gubbio and Nocera, down the mountain of Subasio and so to the confines of Assisi. It was a long, tiring journey on horseback, which aggravated his sickness and increased his pain.

Hearing that he was coming, Bishop Guido, who was a good friend of his and knew how hard and penitential Francis was with himself, invited him into the comfort of the episcopal palace and allowed him to be attended there by a few of his friars. Friars Leo, Rufino, Masseo and Angelo Tancredi, who had been with him when he received the Stigmata and who now watched at his bedside, could do little to alleviate his pain; but it pleased him to have them there and to have them from time to time join in singing the Song of Brother Sun, which he had composed when he had been very ill in the Garden at St. Clare's monastery.

A good doctor, Bongiovanni, came from Arezzo to see the saint while he was at the Bishop's house. Francis asked him: "What thinkest thou, Brother John, of this my sickness of dropsy?"

The doctor guardedly answered: "Brother, it will be well with thee, by God's grace."

But Francis encouraged him: "Tell me the truth, what thinkest thou? Fear not, for by the grace of the Holy Spirit working with me I am so united with my Lord that I am equally content to die or to live."

So the doctor said to him plainly: "Father, according to our physic, thy sickness is incurable and I believe thou wilt die either at the end of September or on the fourth of October."

Then the saint stretched out his hands to the Lord, and said with great reverence, devotion and joy: "Welcome, my Sister Death!"

He then sent for Friars Angelo and Leo, and when they had arrived he asked them to join him in singing once more the Song of Brother Sun. With heavy hearts they joined in as best they could. Just before the last verse, Francis raised his hand as a signal for them to stop. Then, raising his own weak voice, he added: "Praised be Thou, my Lord, for Sister Death of the body from whom no living man can escape. Woe to them who die in mortal sin. Blessed are they who are found in thy most sweet will, for the second death shall not hurt them."

Meanwhile, Friar Elias, the General of the Order, bustled in, disconcerted at hearing all this singing and joy. He remarked: "My dear Father, the people who are thinking of you as a holy person, will be very disedified to hear you carrying on like this. They will say among themselves, 'How is it possible that so holy a person, being so close to death, should show such frivolity?' Death, my dear Father, is a very serious thing, a very sad thing, a prelude to eternity; how can you meet that eventuality singing!"

Francis had his answer ready: "Do you remember that at Foligno you had a vision, and you told me that you had seen that I would not live more than two years? Well, long before you told me that vision I had been still more careful to think every day of my death." And then he added with great spirit: "Brother, let me rejoice in the Lord, in his praises and in my infirmities; for, by the grace of the Holy Spirit working within me, I am so united and joined to my Lord, that of his mercy I am well able to be joyful in Him, the Most High."

September 1226 was drawing to its close. Sister Death was coming nearer to Francis. He expressed an ardent wish to die among his friars at Our Lady of the Angels in the plain below Assisi, where his Order had grown under the protection of the Blessed Mother. Accordingly, a stretcher was provided, the dying man was placed upon it, and Leo, Angelo, Rufino and Messeo carried him gently down the road into the valley. Halfway to their destination, just outside the Lazar House where so many years before he had met and embraced the leper, Francis asked to be put down, and turned round so that he could face Assisi. Supported by Friar Leo, he raised himself a little and looked towards his native town. He could only see it very, very dimly, for he was almost blind. Slowly he raised his arms in a gesture of blessing, and then with his right hand he made a large sign of the Cross, saying: "May the Lord bless thee, O town of Assisi, town faithful to God, for through thee and in thee shall many souls be saved, and in thee many servants of the Most High shall dwell, and of thee many shall be elected to the everlasting kingdom." He rested back on the stretcher and the journey continued.

At the Portiuncula he was laid tenderly down inside one of the small huts that the friars used, and very close to the little chapel of Our Lady. The past and the present were all as one before his mind, all the incidents of his life and the people he had known. He thought first of Clare and her Sisters at St. Damian's and sent them a final blessing. Then he remembered Madonna Jacopa dei Settisoli, Brother Jacopa as he called her, the lady who had befriended him at Rome and who had become a great helper of the friars. She was a long way off, but she ought to know that he was dying. He called Friar Leo to him: "Brother Jacopa, who loves our Order so well, would be very sad if she were not informed that I am near death; we had better write to her." The friar, ready with the pen, took down what Francis dictated: "Dear Sister, if you wish to still see me alive, come right away. Bring a length of linen in which to roll my body and candles for my burial. As well, I would much like you to bring me a little of that marzipan with which you comforted me when I was ill at Rome. God be with you."

While they were deliberating concerning a messenger, there was the noise of horses reining outside and people dismounting. Friars came in to announce with joy that Jacopa was already here! She told them that she heard a voice telling her: "Go and visit your Father Francis; do not delay or you may not find him alive." She had come post haste from Rome with her two sons and a train of servants. "Praise to God," said Francis, "since He has sent our Brother Jacopa. Let her come in, for the regulation against women entering the enclosure is not for her." She knelt at his side, and for some time they prayed together. She showed him exactly what he had asked for, a roll of grey cloth for his burial sheet, candles, incense, and the little sweets that he had wanted. Sadly, however, the latter he could not now taste - he was too far gone.

Thursday and Friday, the first and second of October, and Francis asked that he should die as any poor man without anything whatever - not even in his old habit, which he asked that they take off him and lay him naked on the bare floor. They did this and then covered him decently with the winding sheet. He said to them: "I bless you all as much as I can and more than I can. I have finished my work; may Christ our Saviour teach you how to complete yours."

On the Friday morning he woke with great pain, and thinking it was Thursday, he had in mind the Last Supper. He called all the friars to hm and laid his right hand on the head of each one in turn. He blessed all present and absent and all who would join his Order until the end of time: "And since I cannot speak much for weakness and the pain of my infirmity, I declare to all the brethren present and to come my will and my intention briefly in three phrases: namely, that as a token of my memory, my blessing and my testament, they ever love one another as I have loved and love them; that they ever love poverty, Our Lady; and ever be faithful subjects to the prelates and clergy of the Holy Mother Church."

Then, as Our Lord on the first Holy Thursday night showed his love for the brethren in the breaking of bread, so Francis, in imitation of Him, called for bread, which being brought, he blessed, asked that it be broken since he was too weak to do this himself, and then distributed a piece to every friar present. He then had them read to him the Gospel of St. John where it tells of the Passion of Our Lord. For the rest of that day, Friar Leo and Friar Angelo occasionally sang to him verses of that hymn he loved so much - of Brother Sun. Perhaps it was at this time that he mentioned the place of his burial; esteeming himself to be lowest of all men, he asked that it be on that desolate place known as "The Hill of Hell", where malefactors were executed.

On Saturday, October the third the doctor came to see him and the dying man said to him: "Now tell me that my death is very near, because it is for me the gate of heaven." The doctor assured him that it was so. The rest of the day passed in silence and prayer, but at twilight the Saint asked them to join him in the psalm "With all my voice I cry to the Lord." (Ps. 141). While they were chanting this the Saint of Assisi passed from this life at the words "Bring my soul out of this prison, and then I shall praise your name. Around me the just will assemble because of your goodness to me."

It was about one hour after dusk, the third of October, 1226.

THE BEAUTY OF DEATH

It is a sad state of affairs not to know where you came from, why you are here, and where you are going. But that is the state of a great many people today: eat, drink and be merry, with not even a thought of tomorrow we die. And yet the only absolute certain thing is that each one of us must die. It is, indeed, the only thing worth thinking about, because it is that towards which we are all heading.

An old spirtual axiom has it: "Remember thy last end and thou wilt never sin." It is said that the Carthusians, who never speak, nevertheless always remind one another in passing "Remember death!"

Well, be all that as it may, it presents a pretty gloomy aspect: perhaps the saddest thing in life, surrounded as it is with all the social conventions, is a funeral. You are almost expected to have a long face to suit the occasion - and even to cry. Coffin bearers are the four most lugubrious stalwarts you could hope to meet!

But why should all this be? Dying is just as ordinary an action as being born or eating your dinner. Happily the recent liturgical changes have jolted us to change our outlook and to celebrate our going off to heaven in white as a sign of Resurrection, or purple the colour of penitence, but hardly ever in black, the lack of colour and sign of hopelessness. Strange how black funerals and black requiems came to be the custom, for this was never so with the early Christians.

Do you ever think of these things, and, if so, in what way? The Old Testament tells us "Be thou faithful unto death and I will give thee a crown of life." In the New Testament Our Blessed Lord gives us the wonderful promise touching upon our reception of Himself in the Blessed Sacrament, that He will raise us up at the last day. What more could we want to help us face the separation of death in a valiant and happy state of mind? Francis so faced it, and like all other things in nature it became a Brother and Sister to him.

Convention, and even certain sorts of spirituality impresses upon us too firmly the misguided idea of finality. There is no finality! There is a realization of fulfilment, of a life well spent in the service of God, the Church and one's neighbour; there is the knowledge that here is simply a transference from a subordinate state of existence to an exceedingly higher one, from the natural to the supernatural, from man to God; that there is a movement from a temporary state of trial to an everlasting life of reward and happiness. Consequently when the soul of a good person leaves the body it is surely a day of rejoicing; the early Christians, and the liturgy still, call it the birthday - the birthday into eternal life.

We should not develop a fear of death. There is no terror attached to it. If we have some sort of apprehension as to when or where or how it is going to come upon us, we must train ourselves to "rest in the Lord and wait". Or we may recall the words of a famous preacher, that just as God gives us an appetite for our dinner when we want it, not before and not after, so He will give us an appetite for death just when, in his divine providence, it is to come upon us.

Get the Franciscan outlook. Let it inspire you with greater spiritual efforts in this life and a conscious movement towards Christ, the Eternal Judge. "Be Thou praised, my Lord, of our Sister, Bodily Death, from whom no living man may escape. Woe to those who die in mortal sin! Blessed are they who are found in thy most sweet will, for the second death shall not work them ill. Praise ye and bless my Lord and give Him thanks, and serve Him with great humility."

The most cheering thing about life on earth is that Sister Death is coming to meet us. She will take you gently and you will be welcomed by our sweet Saviour Christ who has loved you, by the Blessed Mother, your patron saint and guardian angel who have prayed for you, watched over you, and helped you through life; you will meet again all those people you have known and loved upon earth, and your knowledge and love will be purer and deeper because imperfection and sin will be non-existent; your mind and spirit, untrammelled and unimpeded by material things will realize intuitively the work and designs of God with men, and you will be full of praise and love for Him and all his creatures. What more glorious to look forward to! What happier day! Ought we not stretch out our arms as did St. Francis: "Welcome Sister Death!"

Blessed Be Thou My Lord

For Our Sister, Bodily Death.

THE ADMONITION
OF
SAINT FRANCIS

GREAT THINGS WE HAVE PROMISED:
GREATER HAVE BEEN PROMISED TO US.

LET US OBSERVE THE FORMER;
LET US ASPIRE TO THE LATTER.

PLEASURE IS SHORT;
PUNISHMENT EVERLASTING:
SUFFERING IS SLIGHT;
GLORY, INFINITE.

MANY ARE CALLED,
FEW ARE CHOSEN:
RETRIBUTION FOR ALL.

BRETHREN, WHILE WE HAVE TIME,
LET US DO GOOD.

cum permisu superiorum